BASKETBALL
★ THE RETURN OF BERNARD KING ★

by Michael Sandler

Consultant: Joe Jones, Men's Basketball Coach
Columbia University, New York, New York

BEARPORT
PUBLISHING COMPANY, INC.

New York, New York

Credits

Editorial development by Judy Nayer

Cover and title page, AP/Wide World Photos; Page 4, Copyright (C) 1985 by "The New York Times Company." Reprinted by permission.; 5, ©Bettmann/CORBIS; 6, ©Bettmann/CORBIS; 7, AP/Wide World Photos; 8, AP/Wide World Photos; 9, John Iacono/Sports Illustrated; 10, John Iacono/Sports Illustrated; 11, John D. Hanlon Sports Illustrated; 12, ©Bettmann/CORBIS; 13, ©Gail Mooney/CORBIS; 14, AP/Wide World Photos; 15, AP/Wide World Photos; 16, Sports Illustrated; 17, Carl Skalak/Sports Illustrated; 18, AP/Wide World Photos; 19 (top), ©Bettmann/CORBIS; 19 (bottom), Steve Stankiewitz; 20, ©Wally McNamee/CORBIS; 21, Dan Cronin/New York Daily News; 22, AP/Wide World Photos; 23, AP/Wide World Photos; 24, ©Bettmann/CORBIS; 25, John Biever Sports Illustrated; 26, AP/Wide World Photos; 27, Chris Marion | springfieldmass.com.

Design and production by
Ralph Cosentino

Library of Congress Cataloging-in-Publication Data

Sandler, Michael.
   Basketball : the return of Bernard King / by Michael Sandler.
      p. cm. — (Upsets & comebacks)
   Includes bibliographical references and index.
   ISBN 1-59716-166-7 (library binding) — ISBN 1-59716-192-6 (pbk.)
   1. King, Bernard, 1956—Juvenile literature. 2. Basketball players—United States—Biography—Juvenile literature. I. Title. II. Series.

   GV884.K56S36 2006
   796.323092 B—dc22
                                        2005026839

For more information, write to Bearport Publishing Company, Inc., 101 Fifth Avenue, Suite 6R, New York, New York 10003. Printed in the United States of America.

1 2 3 4 5 6 7 8 9 10

Table of Contents

One Terrible Moment

He was the most explosive player ever to wear a New York Knicks uniform. He was the most **ferocious** scorer in the **NBA**. The thing that really scared **opponents** was his age! Bernard King was just 28 years old, and getting better every year. No one knew how good he would become. No one could even guess. With Bernard's talent, the sky was the limit.

King Injured as Knicks Lose

By The Associated Press

KANSAS CITY, Mo., March 23 (AP) — The Knicks lost another game tonight, 113-105 to the Kansas City Kings, and in the process may have lost their star scorer, Bernard King, for the season.

King was blocking a driving layup by Reggie Theus of Kansas City with 1 minute 24 seconds left in the game following a turnover by the Knicks. A foul was then called on King, who crashed to the floor and had to be carried off the court with a twisted right knee.

He was walking on crutches after the game.

Mike Sanders, the Knicks' trainer, said the extent of the injury would not be known until King had been examined by the team physician Sunday in New York.

But Coach Hubie Brown was pessimistic. He said after the game that King, the leading scorer in the National Basketball Association, might miss the remainder of the season.

"We are hoping that if it is going to be an operation, that it is not something that will be devastating for him in the future," Brown said.

King leads the league with a 32.8 points-a-game scoring average. He had 37 points at the time he left, 22 of which he scored in the first half.

Otis Thorpe had a career-record 31 points for the Kings and Theus hit two essential free throws in the final 90 seconds.

Theus put the Kings ahead for good, 107-105, with two free throws after the foul by King.

The Knicks failed to score after King left the game.

Theus added four more free throws and Eddie Johnson scored to give the Kings their final winning margin.

Kansas City held a 31-29 lead at the end of the first period and was ahead by 58-53 with 1:39 left in the half when King sparked an 8-2 run with 6 points

Continued on Page 3, Column 3

"It was the most excruciating pain I've ever felt," said Bernard. "While I was in the air, I knew it was over."

Then, in a split second, his future turned dark. The Knicks were playing Kansas City. Bernard ran back to try to block a shot. He slammed his right foot down. As he did, he felt his knee explode!

In Game 2 of the 1986 NBA Championship series, Larry Bird scored 31 points and led his team to victory.

In 1985, the year Bernard hurt his knee, he led the NBA in scoring. His average—32.9 points a game—was almost five points better than that of Boston Celtics' Larry Bird and Chicago Bulls' Michael Jordan.

Brooklyn Ball

Most school yard basketball players in Brooklyn dream of playing for the New York Knicks. Bernard was one of the few who had achieved the dream.

Bernard had learned the game in the playgrounds near his family's apartment in a housing project. On summer evenings, he'd play late into the night. In crowded half court games, he learned how to get his shot off over older, taller players.

Street ball in Brooklyn, New York

Bernard always played to win. In playground ball, losers have to sit and wait for their next turn on the court. Bernard hated to wait.

Stephon Marbury, of the New York Knicks, goes for a shot.

Several famous NBA players have come from Brooklyn. They include Stephon Marbury, Connie Hawkins, Chris Mullin, Lenny Wilkens, Mark Jackson, and World B. Free.

Rising Star

In high school, Bernard's basketball skills won him many college **scholarship** offers. Bernard chose an offer from the University of Tennessee. There he led two different lives.

Off the court, Bernard was a shy, quiet student. In his free time, he often wrote poetry. On the court, he was a different person: **intense**, fierce, and a nearly unstoppable scorer.

Bernard (53) goes for the ball during a college basketball tournament in 1976.

Bernard would crouch down with his back to the basket and then spin and jump at the same time. His shot was so quick that **defenders** never saw it coming. Led by Bernard and fellow New Yorker Ernie Grunfeld, Tennessee became one of the country's toughest college teams.

The "Bernie and Ernie Show" became one of the most feared pairs in college basketball.

 In his first year at Tennessee, Bernard had the best shooting percentage of any college player in the country. He made nearly two-thirds of his shots!

Welcome to the NBA

After college, the NBA's New Jersey Nets **drafted** Bernard. Making the change from college to professional basketball wasn't easy. In college, Bernard played 30 games a year. Now he was playing 80. Practices were hard. Traveling was hard. Meeting everyone's **expectations** was even harder.

Bernard joined the Nets in 1977.

New Jersey had recently traded away their star, the **legendary** dunker Julius "Dr. J" Erving. Bernard was taking his place on the team. Taking over Dr. J's role was an almost impossible challenge.

Bernard did his best. He showed sparks of greatness. At the season's end, he was second in the voting for **rookie** of the year.

No one could replace Dr. J (32), the greatest dunker in basketball history.

In his rookie year, Bernard led the Nets in scoring. He averaged 24 points a game.

Coming Home

Over the next few seasons, though, Bernard didn't get better. He was still a young man, learning how to be an adult. He wasn't always **focused** on basketball.

Bernard was traded from team to team. First he went to Utah, then Golden State, and finally in 1982 to the New York Knicks.

Now Bernard was back home. He was playing for the team he had rooted for as a boy. He was playing in front of his family and friends. He was playing just a subway ride away from the playgrounds where he learned the game.

In New York, Bernard changed. He became a king.

Madison Square Garden is a short ride across the East River from the Brooklyn neighborhood where Bernard grew up.

Two Nights in Texas

Playing in New York energized Bernard. His game took off. During his second season with the Knicks, Bernard made history during a Texas **road trip**. The first stop was San Antonio.

Bernard was on fire. He couldn't miss a shot. San Antonio players tried everything, but no one could stop him. Bernard scored 50 points in that one game.

Bernard dribbles down the court during his second 50-point game.

After Bernard scored 50 points in back-to-back games, Knicks coach Hubie Brown told reporters, "I've never seen anything like it. Never. There are just no words to describe him."

The next night, against the Dallas Mavericks, Bernard gave a repeat performance. He shot the ball sideways and backwards. Every ball he tossed into the air flew into the hoop. He scored 50 points again!

Afterward, Bernard was **humble**. "The important thing was that we won these two nights," he said.

It had been 20 years since an NBA player had scored 50 points on back-to-back nights.

King of the Court

In 1984, the Knicks rolled into a **playoff** battle with the Detroit Pistons. Bernard was too much for them. Despite injured fingers, he scored 40 points, four games in a row. Then the Knicks moved on to play Boston.

Few thought the series would be close. Led by Larry Bird, the Boston Celtics were basketball's best team. They were determined to stop Bernard.

Bernard (30) watches as a player on the Pistons tries to score.

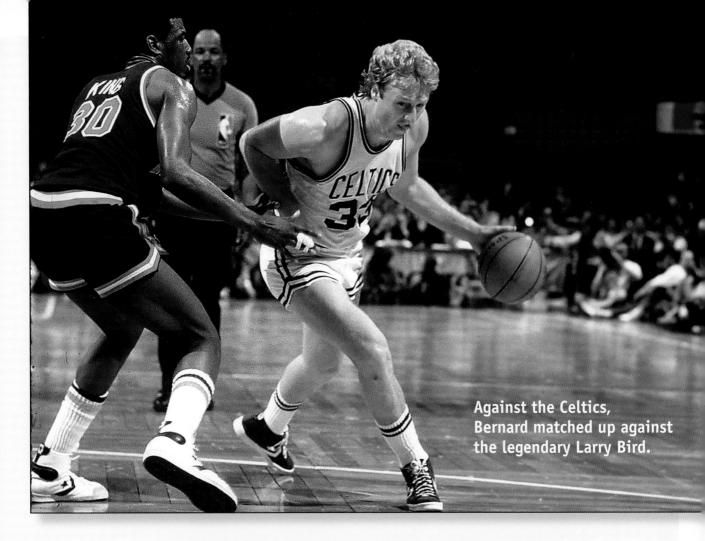

Against the Celtics, Bernard matched up against the legendary Larry Bird.

Whenever Bernard got the ball, Celtics players surrounded him. It didn't matter. Bernard shot around them and over them. Impossible **jumpers** rained down into the hoop.

The Knicks thrilled their fans by almost winning the series. Bernard had been incredible!

Bernard's 42.6-point scoring average against Detroit was an NBA record.

Dreams and Nightmares

The following season, Bernard kept getting even better. He took his game to a level few players had ever reached. One night he scored 55 points. Another night he scored 60.

In March, however, Bernard's dream season came to a horrible end when his knee collapsed. As he crumpled to the court, Bernard knew it was bad.

"No one needed to tell me it was probably over," Bernard said.

Bernard's 60-point game was a New York Knicks record.

Doctors **confirmed** his fears. He had torn his anterior cruciate ligament (ACL). Few athletes had ever returned from this kind of injury. None had returned to greatness. Most doctors thought Bernard's career was over.

Bernard at a press conference discussing his injury

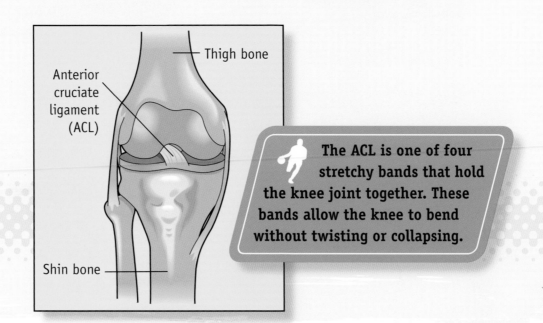

Thigh bone

Anterior cruciate ligament (ACL)

Shin bone

The ACL is one of four stretchy bands that hold the knee joint together. These bands allow the knee to bend without twisting or collapsing.

The Long Road Back

Knicks' doctor Norman Scott did his best to undo the damage. In a long operation, he repaired the torn ligament. Afterward, Bernard lay in a hospital bed. He had 40 metal staples in his knee.

Questions ran through Bernard's mind. Would he be as fast? Would he be as strong? Could a rebuilt knee stand up to the pounding of an 82-game NBA season?

Patrick Ewing (33) before being drafted by the Knicks.

Shortly after Bernard's operation, the Knicks drafted the great college **center** Patrick Ewing. Bernard cried when he heard the news. He knew he might never get the chance to play with Patrick.

Bernard working out after his knee operation

Bernard wasn't going to quit until he found out. For nearly two years, he worked out alone, without teammates, reporters, or distractions. He lifted weights. He ran. He swam. Slowly, he worked the knee into shape.

Good-bye, Knicks

With just six games left in the 1987 season, Bernard walked onto the court. Knicks' fans stood and cheered. They had waited a long time. Their hero had returned.

Bernard looked like the same player. There was only one difference. His knee was wrapped in a brace.

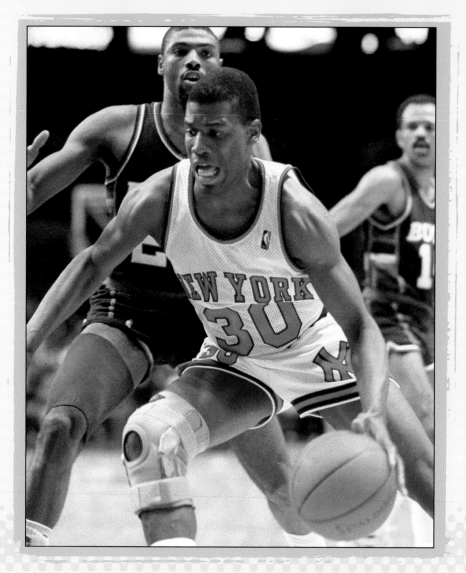

Bernard in his first game back after his knee operation

Bernard
scored 20
points in his
second game
back.

Of course, Bernard wasn't the same. He was rusty. He was slow. It was clear, however, that he could still play ball. Could he become a star again?

Fans believed in Bernard. Team officials, however, didn't. At season's end, the team let him go. Bernard's career as a Knick was over.

Bernard never got a chance to play with Patrick Ewing. During Bernard's brief return with the Knicks, Patrick was out with an injury.

Wanted in Washington

Another team, however, was willing to give Bernard a chance. He signed on with the Washington Bullets (now the Wizards).

Starting over wasn't easy. Bernard's knee was better, but it wasn't the same as before. He didn't have the same strength. He didn't have the same explosive quickness.

Bernard in a Bullets uniform

24

So Bernard set about teaching himself new ways to score. His first season back he averaged 17 points. In each season that followed, his scoring increased. He averaged 20, 22, and then 28 points a game. Doctors had said coming back would take a miracle. Bernard was making the miracle happen.

In 1991, Bernard was third in the league in scoring, after Michael Jordan and Karl Malone.

A Moment to Be Proud

In 1991, Bernard finally returned to the NBA **All-Star** team. Six years had passed since the tragic night in Kansas City. Six years had passed since the moment his career seemed to end. The feeling was magical.

"It was an unreal moment," Bernard remembers. "I didn't want to just come back. I wanted to come back as an All-Star."

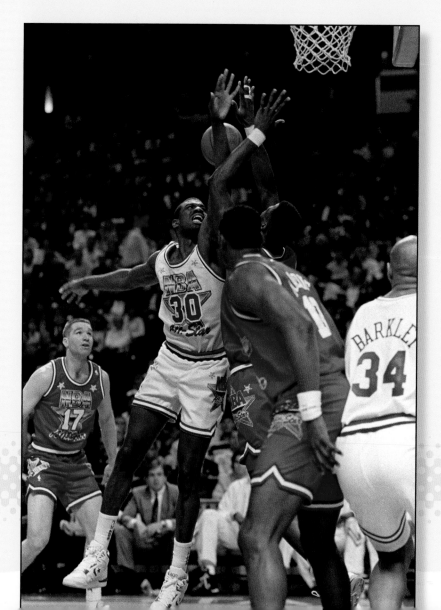

Bernard (30) reaches for the ball during the All-Star game.

He had. Two years later, Bernard retired. He never looked back at the years lost to injury. He never regretted what might have been.

"I played like a kid out of Brooklyn who loved the Knicks. I lived a dream," he says.

The Basketball Hall of Fame in Springfield, Massachusetts

To enter basketball's Hall of Fame, a player must first be chosen as a finalist by a group of basketball experts. In 2004 and 2005, Bernard was named a finalist. If elected, Bernard will join the special few who are considered the best ever to play the game.

Just the Facts

More About Basketball and Bernard King

★ **Back-to-Back Fifties**—Only six other players in NBA history have recorded back-to-back 50-point games. These players are Rick Barry, Elgin Baylor, Wilt Chamberlain, Allen Iverson, Antawn Jamison, and Michael Jordan.

★ **Power Turkey**—After scoring 50 points against San Antonio, Bernard wanted to do everything the same before his next game. So he had the same meal—a turkey sandwich and a milk shake. "I wasn't taking any chances," King said. "I ate the same meal the day before and scored 50."

Timeline

This timeline shows some important events in the life and career of Bernard King.

★ **1956**
Bernard is born in Brooklyn, New York.

★ **1977**
Bernard is drafted by the Nets.

1956   **1962**   **1968**   **1974**   **1980**

★ **1974**
Bernard joins the University of Tennessee basketball team.

★ **Family Affair**—While Bernard was in high school, he wasn't even considered the best basketball player in his family. His little brother, Albert, was often called the nation's best high school basketball player. Though Albert went on to a solid NBA career, he never achieved the same success as Bernard.

★ **Thanks, Doc**—Who was the first person Bernard called when he made it back to the All-Star Game in 1991? The doctor who made it possible! Bernard called Dr. Norman Scott and invited him to the game.

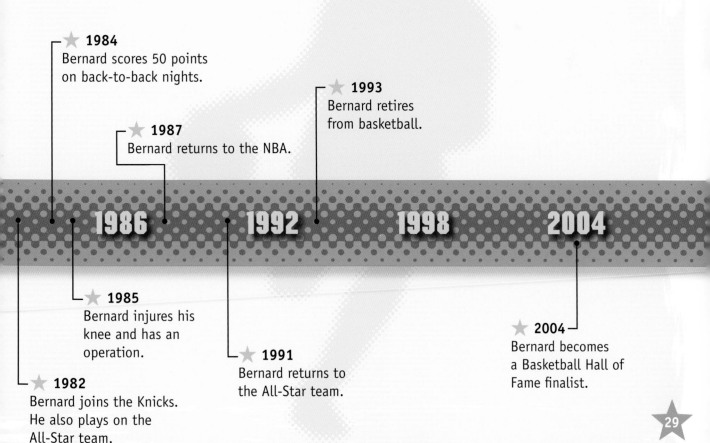

★ **1984**
Bernard scores 50 points on back-to-back nights.

★ **1993**
Bernard retires from basketball.

★ **1987**
Bernard returns to the NBA.

1986   **1992**   **1998**   **2004**

★ **1985**
Bernard injures his knee and has an operation.

★ **2004**
Bernard becomes a Basketball Hall of Fame finalist.

★ **1991**
Bernard returns to the All-Star team.

★ **1982**
Bernard joins the Knicks. He also plays on the All-Star team.

Glossary

All-Star (AWL-STAR) a game or team that matches the best NBA players from the East Coast teams against the best NBA players from the West Coast teams

center (SEN-tur) one of the standard positions on a basketball team, usually held by the tallest player

confirmed (kuhn-FURMD) let a person know that something is true

defenders (di-FEN-durz) players in the act of trying to stop other players from scoring

drafted (DRAFT-id) chosen or picked to play for a team

expectations (*ek*-spek-TAY-shunz) people's thoughts about what should happen

ferocious (fuh-ROH-shuhss) fierce; unstoppable

focused (FOH-kuhssd) able to keep one's concentration on something

humble (HUHM-buhl) not boastful

intense (in-TENSS) very strong; always serious and determined

jumpers (JUHM-purz) shots released into the air after a player's feet have left the ground

legendary (LEJ-uhn-der-ee) extremely well known; famous

NBA National Basketball Association; a professional basketball league that has 27 teams in the United States and two teams in Canada

opponents (uh-POH-nuhntz) athletes one plays against in a sporting event

playoff (PLAY-awf) a series of games played to determine a championship

road trip (ROHD TRIP) a series of games in which a team plays away from home, traveling from town to town

rookie (RUK-ee) a first-year player

scholarship (SKOL-ur-ship) a grant of money for a person to attend school

Bibliography

Basketball Digest

New York *Daily News*

New York Post

The New York Times

Shouler, Ken, Bob Ryan, Sam Smith, Leonard Koppett, and Bob Bellottio. *Total Basketball: The Ultimate Basketball Encyclopedia.* Toronto: SportClassic Books Publishing (2003).

www.nba.com

Read More

Burleigh, Robert. *Hoops.* New York: Voyager Books (2001).

Coy, John. *Strong to the Hoop.* New York: Lee & Low (2003).

Hareas, John. *Basketball.* New York: DK Publishing (2003).

Smith Jr., Charles R. *Hoop Kings.* Cambridge, MA: Candlewick (2004).

Learn More Online

Visit these Web sites to learn more about basketball, Bernard King, and the NBA:

www.hickoksports.com/biograph/kingbernard.shtml

www.hoophall.com/

www.nba.com/history/players/kingb_bio.html

Index

About the Author

Michael Sandler lives in Brooklyn, New York. He has written numerous books on sports for children and young adults. Like many New York fans, he only wishes Bernard and Patrick had gotten their chance to play together for the Knicks.